LOOKING FOR SMOKE:
Adventures of an Aerial Observer

By JB Poet

I spent several summers flying with a pilot in a small plane over the
Willamette National Forest looking for Wild Fires.
This book gives an account of some of my memories from that job.

See also, *Fifteen Years at Imnaha Guard Station,* a book I wrote about being a fireman
on the Rogue River National Forest in southern Oregon in the 1970s and 80s.
There my wife and I raised four outstanding sons.
Xlibris published it and you can find it on their web site: Xlibris.com

Dedicated to:

Jacob Lee Thompson aka *Squeek*
Andrew Ray Thompson aka *Boca*

At one month, when I first saw him, Jacob seldom cried. But when he was hungry
his cry sounded like a mouse. He became *Squeek*.

A year and a half later Andrew came along. After he developed the habit of opening his mouth like a bird wanting food,
I asked a friend for the Spanish word for mouth. Andrew became *Boca*.

Both boys show enormous love for each other and for me! They are more like
identical twins than most identical twins.

Squeek and Boca lived with me for the first few years of their lives, 24/7.
They went everywhere with their *Papa*. I love them dearly!

*I want to thank Dave Coplin for editing,
photographs and encouragement. A debt is also owed to Nate Meyer,
manager of the McKenzie Field Jerry's Home Improvement Store,
for his help in editing and corrections. Don Allen
graciously contributed several fine photographs.*

*I am especially thankful for the help and encouragement of Glenda Tuttle,
Grandma of Squeek and Boca.*

Library of Congress Control Number: 2005911444
ISBN: Softcover   978-1-4257-0633-3
        Hardcover   978-1-4257-0823-8
        EBook   978-1-4771-7480-7

Cover Photo:
Circling Coffin Mountain Lookout in 85 Golf.
Don Allen Photo.

Print information available on the last page.

Rev. date: 07/25/2019

To order additional copies of this book, contact:
Xlibris
1-888-795-4274
www.Xlibris.com
Orders@Xlibris.com

Boca and Squeek liked to go with Papa to cut firewood.
This photo was taken in 2001

High Altitude Bombing

I only did it once. Don't know why, but one day I plunked down enough quarters to buy six newspapers at the airport before our flight. Then as we approached Coffin Mountain Lookout I told my pilot, Jerry Pierce, "Stay high. I want to do it from altitude."

My instructions were not clear. As we made our approach at about 7,500 feet I began to prepare the plastic bags. (Coffin's elevation is 5,771 feet.) Jerry thought I wanted him to dive bomb. Suddenly I felt my stomach do a flip and looked out the windshield to see Coffin Mountain. I warned him just in time and we leveled off.

I held all of the papers, in plastic bags, out of the window. I had each one between two different fingers, so was using both hands. I began to release one paper at a time at intervals of one second or less.

Not much wiggle room for hitting Coffin with a newspaper.

I couldn't see the lookout. It was almost directly beneath the plane. I could only guess when the time was right and hope Jerry had put us on a direct line above.

The papers were gone. We didn't even circle to watch the result. We just continued our route.

When we flew well above the mountain like this Don didn't expect any C.A.R.E. packages at his remote retreat. This would especially be true when we went straight on. In that first year we didn't say much on the radio. Don would send me a "damage report" when the next visitor took out his mail. This usually was about two weeks.

Don's report: "I thought you weren't going to drop anything because you were so high. Then as I was watching you disappear to the north I heard a distant 'plop.' It came from over the edge to the south. Then there was a closer 'plop,' followed quickly by a loud one as a paper landed just beside the lookout. Before I could get on the catwalk to look there was another 'plop' just on the north side of the structure. Then I heard a faint 'plop' over the edge of the north cliff."

That was only five. I guess one landed too early or too late.

The experiment was a huge success. I was tickled that I surprised him, flying so far above. I was really surprised that we straddled the building! It's true. Better to be lucky than good!

In the photo above the papers landed left to right. Turn pages to the first "Go Ducks" photograph. The papers landed right to left.

Background

Detection is the first part of fighting wild fire. The point is to find (detect) the fire as early as possible so that suppression crews can put it out before it gets large and cannot be controlled without massive resources.

There has been a debate about Forest Service efforts to prevent and control wildfire fire. One theory says this is responsible for fuel buildup that in recent years has resulted in catastrophic fires. Part of this may be true. But if that were the general case one would expect to find no huge destructive fires in the past. The opposite is true.

Consider the Tillamook Burn. In four major fires over 18 years beginning in 1933, the coast range of Oregon suffered a fire that changed the economy of an entire state for years. Over 350,000 acres were burned with a loss of more than 13,000,000,000 board feet of timber. That's Billions, with a "B". Fire Prevention and control were just beginning to have some effect. See http://www.tillamoo.com/burn.html)

Consider the "Idaho Fires of 1910," when the fire control efforts of the Forest Service were still in their baby stages. Called "The largest forest fire in American history," three million acres were burning at one time. Most of that destruction came in just six hours! Lost in the Idaho tragedy is the fact that huge fires also burned in Washington and Oregon at the same time. Dozens of people lost their lives. (See http://www.idahoforests.org/fires.htm)

Consider the Peshtigo Fire in1871, years before the Forest Service was even an idea. It is estimated that between 1,200 and 2,400 people died. An entire town was consumed, plus many small communities and farms. This was at the same time as the Chicago Fire, but not nearly as well covered by the press. (See http://www.peshtigofire.info/.)

These fires occurred primarily because weather conditions were just right. It was not "fuel buildup," but high winds and low humidity. Catastrophic fires today occur during periods of unusually high winds and low humidity.

In the early years of the Forest Service detection usually meant strategically placed lookouts on the tops of mountains and often in towers. In the early 1900s an enterprising lookout with experience as a sailor built his own "tower" by drilling holes in a large tree and making a spiral staircase to the top. He then constructed a platform on which to sit. Better him than me!

After World War II the use of aircraft as a detection platform began to grow. The Willamette National Forest was among the pioneers, with aircraft flying out of McKenzie Field in Springfield, Oregon, to check the forests along the crest of the Cascades. In the late 1960s Ron Kintzley was one of the innovating Aerial Observers. I hope he writes a book about his experiences one day. He has many exciting stories to tell!

Milt Ruberg owned McKenzie Field and McKenzie Flying Service. Sometime in the early 1970s McKenzie field became too small and Milt moved his operation to Mahon Sweet Airport north of Eugene. Milt slowly sold off parcels of ground that had once been McKenzie Field.

Jerry Orem and his wife Merle started Jerry's Home Improvement store. Their first store was just south of where the Mahlon Sweet Airport is located. This was in 1961. By the late 1990s it had grown and a huge store was built nearby on Highway 99 at the edge of Eugene. It is believed to be one of the largest Home Improvement stores in North America.

In January 2003 Jerry's opened their second store in the middle of the McKenzie Field airstrip, between a Wal-Mart store and a K-Mart building. The front entrance to Jerry's sits very close to the edge of the old airstrip and just about midway along it's length.

Dennis Orem, the son of Jerry and Merle who started "Jerry's," and his wife Sharon, named this the McKenzie Field Store in reference to the former airport.

Jerry's Home Improvement store now occupies part of the old McKenzie airstrip. The runway ran near the front of the store.

A New Job

Beginning in the early 1960s I worked for the Forest Service on The Rogue River National Forest in Southern Oregon during the summers. I was pasturing a small church and attending college in Ashland at first. Then I began teaching school, so the tradition continued. I wrote about a big part of those summers in the book, *Fifteen Years at Imnaha Guard Station*, published in 2005 by Xlibris.

In 1986 I moved to the Willamette National Forest, near Eugene. I had been advised the position of a fire guard at Imnaha was going to be eliminated.

I had traded fire prevention slides with Ron Kintzley in the early 1980s. Now I went to him in Lowell and asked about a job. He was the AFMO (Assistant Fire Management Officer) for the Lowell District. He was also in charge of Aerial Detection for the entire Willamette, which consisted of five districts and is the largest National Forest in Oregon. (The second year Sara Robertson became the leader of the Observer program, another of my outstanding supervisors.)

Ron worked closely with the Fire Staff at the Supervisors Office in Eugene. The Fire Management Officer there was none other than Woody Williams, whom I had met while working on the Rogue. I wrote about him in my book mentioned above. Woody remembered me and between the two of them I was assured of a transfer to the Willamette.

John Robison started off as a smoke jumper. When I went to Lowell he was the FMO. Later he moved to the Supervisor's Office in Eugene and was part of the Fire Staff there while I was a Dispatcher when my Observer days were over. Many folks from one location kept popping up at another location in my Forest Service career. As I have mentioned before, with one exception in Butte Falls, all my supervisors in schools and in the Forest Service have been outstanding individuals! Each of them helped me to achieve.

My job on the Willamette would be that of an Aerial Observer. There were several staffed lookouts on the Willamette, but Woody and Ron believed in using aircraft to augment those fixed detection locations. I reported to Lowell in June when school was out and began my training. I explain the first day on this job in my book, *Fifteen Years at Imnaha Guard Station*.

In Lowell my first task was to build my own maps file. This consisted of a regular forest map cut into manageable sections and covered in plastic. These were used as an "over all" guide. There were seven maps in all fitting on four two sided 18" by 18" sheets. That was as big as one could easily handle in the cockpit of an airplane.

My second task was the construction of a map book. Each page was an 8 1/2 by 11 view of just one township. It allowed one to pinpoint a location by using contour lines as well as watercourses and road systems. The book was organized to mesh with the larger map sheets, so one could quickly locate the correct "zoom in" page.

Breaking Tradition

McKenzie Flying Service had the contract to provide planes and pilots for many years. Milt Ruberg seemed to feel it was his civic responsibility to bid so low on the contract to provide pilots and planes for Aerial Detection that it was always awarded to him.

According to the contract, McKenzie Flying Service had a minimum of one airplane ready for use depending on the fire weather forecast for the following day. Personnel at Lowell Ranger Station and the McKenzie Flying Service office at Mahlon Sweet Airport coordinated this.

In 1985 another small company underbid McKenzie Flying Service, barely. What a shock. This meant that for the 1986 summer observers would fly out of Cottage Grove or Oakridge. It was a nightmare of logistics. More important, there were safety concerns.

Sherry's Shock

That summer Sherry Bernard was also a rookie Observer. Since she was already an employee at Oakridge and didn't have to complete a school year she was through with her training and map bookwork when I arrived. Steve Heath was one of the current Observers who helped train her. He then went on to get his pilots license a year or so later. On her first solo flight with just her and a pilot things did not go well.

As they were flying along the crest the engine began to miss. The pilot said, "Not to worry. It's probably just a bit of icing," and pulled on the "carb heat." It settled some, but soon missed again. Sherry made the decision to abort the flight and head to the airport. They didn't make it.

As they kept losing altitude coming west it soon became apparent the airport was beyond reach. There *was* an open field that was inviting, right beside I-105 in Springfield, just south of the Kingsford Briquette plant. Fortunately the plane had recently been in Alaska and sported balloon tires. They made a rough but safe landing in the field.

An FAA investigation revealed two problems. First of all the pilot had *not* checked the fuel. He assumed there was enough for the trip but when they landed the tanks were already empty.

Second, when the earlier Forest Service inspection was done, the carrier was required to replace all fuel lines. A mechanic had failed to lubricate one of the lines when he replaced it and the tubing cut into the softer hose. It created a "clapper valve" so that when the fuel demand was small things were fine but when the engine asked for more gasoline the flap of tubing was sucked down tight and starved the engine.

If that had *not* happened Sherry and her pilot no doubt would have run out of fuel somewhere far from any landing zone. It could not have ended well.

50 Mike

...n later, happier times, Sherry flies toward south and Middle ...ister in 74 Hotel.

Woody Williams made the decision that McKenzie Flying Service would take over the contract because of obvious safety violations. Until the kinks were worked out in a couple of weeks, I flew with the "new" contractor. Nearly all of my first dozen flights were from Oakridge airport. I thought it was normal for the stall warning to go off when you were taking off! By comparison Mahlon Sweet had huge runways and no scary crosswinds!

The Aircraft

The planes we used most often were 85 Golf and 74 Hotel. These were the call signs for air traffic controllers, which came from the last three characters of the FAA tail number. ("Eight Five Golf" and "Seven four Hotel.") To USFS dispatchers I was "Patrol Plane Five," Sherry was "Patrol Plane Three" and later my son, John, became "Patrol Plane Six."

The plane I flew in most often was 85 Golf. It was 12-volt. Sherry usually took 74 Hotel, a 24-volt plane. More than once I had to go back to the terminal to exchange radios when the pilot said, "Oh, didn't you know we would be flying this one today?"

It was not easy to get in-flight photos of the planes. Often we would communicate on our way out to patrol and be a mile apart. Couldn't see each other. Pilots like it that way. So if we wanted pictures the two pilots would be in constant radio contact and the two observers also. It wasn't often we were able to arrange it from a logistics standpoint.

These aircraft are Cessna 182 Skylanes. This means they had 230 HP engines, variable pitch propellers and flaps for more safety, among other features.

The Pilots

McKenzie Flying Service, depending on who was available and who wanted to fly us, assigned pilots. But when two observers were going up at the same time we developed trends. Even though I usually went with Dave Coplin or Dave Soha, I had confidence in all of the flyers. I got along well with the Daves. They had a lot of experience. Sherry liked to go with Jay Lohner.

The contract stated a pilot had to have 1,500 hours of flying time and specified that 500 hours had to be mountain flying. All of McKenzie's pilots were over qualified. Al Quinby was an excellent United Airlines pilot who liked to get out and do some "recreational work" once in a while. All were instructors, as McKenzie was not only a charter service but a private pilot school as well.

Dave Soha had over 10,000 hours in a B-52! I felt comfortable with all of our pilots. They were all safety conscious. The Daves were exceptional. We often talked about what requirements a "landing zone" in the mountains would have. There were thousands of miles of roads at lower elevations, and an occasional meadow with unknown firmness near the crest.

Dave Soha driving 85 Golf.

Sometimes Soha would reach over and cut the power and say, "Bob, we just lost the engine. Where can we set down?" I might reply with, "A ridge top road just passed beneath us." He would put the plane into a slow gentle circle and check out my suggestion.

As we lined up and viewed the road from a better angle he would apply power and report. Usually it was, "We would walk away from that one."

Beside the Daves, Al and Jay, other pilots I flew with were, Jerry Pierce and Bob Schmidt.

I flew many missions that June checking prescribed burns with an experienced observer. Finally I was ready to "solo." Even though it was a bit of a nerve wringer, the pilots were so experienced that it was almost impossible to goof things up too badly.

First Smoke

There is a curious thing about smoke. Whether you are in a lookout tower or an aircraft, often you "think" you might have a smoke. However, when an honest to goodness smoke pops up there is no doubt. On a north zone flight after a lightning storm I saw a small whiff near Jump Off Joe, south and a little west of Iron Mountain Lookout. It was fairly easy to get a correct "legal location" on it because of nearby logging units, which followed section lines.

Each smoke was turned in only after the observer had accurately located the spot with township, range, section, quarter section and quarter of a quarter. That was before accurate GPS units were available. I used to teach my seventh and eighth grade math students how to find a spot given the legal and how to write a legal of a given physical feature. My sons could all locate radio reported legals on the guard station wall map before they could read and write.

But it is *much* different starting from zero — having a smoke hundreds or thousands of feet below you. The map in your lap keeps changing positions as the plane circles. The first thing to do was climb to make certain you had the overall picture accurately. Then your pilot drops lower as you narrow the plot to at least a section. Finally you went as low as he felt comfortable so that you could look for additional information, such as access, water sources nearby, hazards or fuel problems. It was always a team operation.

It was a challenge to get information to the dispatcher as quickly as possible so crews could be underway. And you wanted to beat any other reports, especially from a mountain top lookout. They had sharp eyes!

Combine that with the desire to *never* report a fire and then have to change the legal location because of making an error and it could be a nerve wracking few minutes.

Newspaper Delivery

Part of our mission was to learn and practice dropping messages so that we could communicate with a crew on the ground when radio contact was not possible. We had sand weighted packs designed for this. They were even equipped with several yards of red streamer to make them more visible to folks on the ground. I didn't want to waste those so decided to try dropping "messages" to lookouts in other forms.

on Allen waves from the catwalk of Coffin Mountain Lookout.

This came about in great part because of my experience with Jack Hamilton when we dropped a large sack of bubble gum to a youth camp near Prospect, Oregon, in the 1960s. (This event is chronicled in my book, *Fifteen Years at Imnaha Guard Station*.)

My first attempt was a spur of the moment choice. I had a candy bar with me and I suggested to my pilot, Dave Soha, that we try to get it to Don Allen on Coffin Mountain. I told him what I thought would work. He had some suggestions.

It was decided we would fly right over the lookout and I would signal him to tip the plane on its right wing when I thought we were just about in position. There is considerable time when the terrain and lookout, below and in front of you, is not visible.

I held the package out of the window. If we were on a good line I would then have a few seconds to decide if the package had a chance of getting close as we flew in a slight curve over the mountaintop. We very seldom had to go around. Remember the aircraft was hundreds of feet above the target and moving somewhere near 135 mph. We rapidly developed a smooth working procedure. The pilots were good!

85 Golf didn't have an opening window on the passenger side.

I had to force my arm out of the door. The wind pressure was fierce. It was a fairly small sacrifice.

That first effort was amazing. I released the bar as we passed over the lookout. It was too small to see as it fell to earth. I wondered if it came close. We continued on our route without saying anything on the radio.

A few minutes later the radio crackled. "Patrol Plane 5, this is Coffin Mountain." I answered and Don made the terse comment. "It landed on the roof."

At that time the districts did the fire dispatching. The Patrol Planes had to check in when we crossed into District territory and let them know when we were leaving. It didn't seem prudent to advertise what we were doing with airdrops, even though guidelines for the Observers said to practice message drops.

There was a very short pause and the Detroit Dispatcher called Coffin Mountain. "*What* landed on the roof?" Don responded with just two words, "Candy bar." Then there was silence. Never heard a word about it later.

In 85 Golf, flaps down, preparing for a drop to Coffin.

If that first attempt had not been on target, I would not have known whether to let loose sooner or later. Fortunately I was lucky! That was the start of some amazing feats with Patrol Plane 5 and Coffin Mountain. I certainly didn't drop something on every trip. Not even half of the time. I did try to get Don a current Eugene Register Guard newspaper whenever I could, especially on early morning flights. There weren't many of these.

When there was a thunderstorm late in the day or over night, Patrol Planes were put up at or shortly after daylight to catch smokes while the humidity was still high. They tended to put up more smoke then compared to later in the morning when they heated up. Fires spread rapidly in afternoon heat. We wanted to find them when they were small.

One Saturday morning I grabbed a newspaper at the airport and put it in a plastic barf bag like I normally did. Soha and I had been assigned the North Zone. We flew without incident until we approached Coffin Mountain and Dave lined up on the lookout. As happened many times, there was no radio traffic. Don would write letters to me and explain where the papers landed. This usually took a week or two.

This time his report was classic. He wrote that early in the morning a family had hiked the 2 1/2 miles to the lookout. The man was thrilled with the view and Don's job. He told him, "This is a perfect job. I would *love* to do this." Then he paused and said, "But I just couldn't get along without my newspaper."

Sunrise on an early morning flight. The Three Sisters are to the left.

Don didn't say anything about getting papers once in a while, but only two or three minutes later he heard the drone of 85 Golf. He still didn't say anything. Shortly there was a firm "plop" — right on the front step. Don nonchalantly walked out and picked up the bagged Register Guard.

The man was incredulous. He looked at his watch and exclaimed, "I don't get my paper in Eugene this early on Saturday. And it often doesn't even make the porch!" That was probably our most accurate drop, but usually they were within a few yards of the structure. If I missed very far the papers ended up hundreds of feet away, over the side of the steep cliffs.

Correcting for Wind

I didn't always do that so well. When weather conditions brought high pressure to eastern Oregon and a low off the coast, strong east winds came through the Cascade passes. Coffin Mountain is just north of Santiam Pass, so it gets the brunt of these gales — sometimes more than 70 mph. This is also a critical time for fires since east winds bring extremely low humidity.

One trip during east wind conditions I planned to drop a newspaper to Don. It is obvious to us in the plane when the wind is blowing. Lots of bumps. So Dave altered our drop route so we were flying directly into the wind. As we approached the Lookout it seemed like we were crawling. With flaps down and going into 60+ mph wind our ground speed was very slow!

85 Golf just after a drop to Coffin Mountain. Don Allen photo.

I decided to wait much longer than usual to drop because I thought the paper's trajectory would be impeded. I was actually looking back at the rock cliff on the east side of the lookout when I finally released.

Don told me later the wind had taken the paper clear to the opposite end of the flat top area, past the helispot and over the west edge. That's got to be at least 300 meters west of where it was released! (Note photographs next page!)

Carpet Bombing

Another time I prepared a paper like I always did. I rolled it and put it in a barf bag. When released, the paper would unroll against the bag and create a parachute effect. I seldom tied it. This time, however as I released the paper things were different. My pilots always turned the plane to the right so I could look behind and watch the progress of each drop. (I never could figure out how they could do that. If I were flying the plane we would have turned left so I, the pilot, could observe!)

This time when I looked back all I saw was a huge cloud of white. The wind had sucked the paper out of the bag and neatly separated every sheet without tearing it. Behind us was a blizzard of newsprint slowly drifting earthward. I suspect we may have been off the district by the time they all got to the ground! Oh, well. Newspaper makes excellent mulch.

Don was a Duck Fan. He couldn't go to the games, but every August and September game day he would give one-line updates of the football game score on the radio — for those in the field without commercial radio capabilities. (And maybe just a bit to poke good-natured fun at Beaver Fans.)

Once in a while he would soften and include an OSU score. Often as we headed out for a Saturday flight I took pictures of Autzen Stadium filling up on game day. When it was an afternoon flight I could even catch the game in progress. After 9/11 these photos would not be possible. Air space around crowds like that is restricted.

One Saturday I had a surprise when I flew over Coffin, so I circled and took a few photos. Don had climbed onto the roof and using 8 1/2 by 11 notebook paper had spelled out "Go Ducks" on the flat surface. He had to weight the papers with rocks to keep them from being blown away. After my flight he took them down.

I had a teacher friend who was a part time Sports Writer for the Eugene Register Guard. I showed him a couple of the photos and he took them to his second job. The Guard was "this close" to printing one on the front page of the Friday paper before a home game when some big news story broke and they delayed the "human interest story." Human interest didn't return to the Guard that season.

Coffin Mountain Lookout decorated for a University of Oregon game day.

Nice sign, but not many folks got to see it!

A Saturday morning and Autzen Stadium is filling up for an afternoon game.

Another Saturday and the game is in progress.

Wind Speed and Direction

I often wondered what folks on the ground thought about our skills. Once in a while I would be asked by a burn boss on the ground as we were checking out his unit, "What's the wind speed and direction up there?" Even the Dispatcher in Eugene would sometimes ask that question.

What did they think, that I could wet my finger and stick it out the window? Nevertheless, we did give them a reading after a few moments.

Smart pilots! They would check air speed as given by a device on the skin of the plane. Then they would compare it to the speed given by the Loran Unit, an electronic device before GPS that fairly accurately gave a constant update of Lat/Long (Latitude and Longitude) and ground speed as we were constantly changing position.

As we flew in a large circle the pilot could determine where the difference was most pronounced, subtract the two and give a pretty accurate wind speed and direction. Did those folks on the ground think we were pulling their leg some times?

Bees

One 1988 August day I asked Don how he was doing. By this time we had centralized dispatch in Eugene and we checked in with lookouts on each flight. Don replied he was doing fine, that he hadn't been stung yet that day. It was the first day in about a week that he hadn't been stung at least once, usually when he went to the weather station a few yards from the lookout to record conditions.

The next trip I carried a couple of empty plastic milk jugs. I had used a heated pencil tip to poke several holes in the containers. Don was to put some "meat bait" inside and then put the jugs outside. The bees crawl inside easily smelling the meat. But with the holes poked from the outside it was difficult for them to find their way back out.

I tied the jugs together with a short cord and tried to guess how they would descend. I don't know how close I got, but Don recovered them quickly. The theory was he would have to empty the jugs in a week or so.

He called me on the radio about 45 minutes later, while we were still on the north zone. He said only, "Bob, I've already had to empty the jug. It was about 3/4 full!" That was a serious bee problem.

When I returned to the airport I contacted a friend who knew someone in the pest control business. He gave me some powerful stuff he said would fix the problem. I was to mix a small amount with some cat food and put it out for the yellow jackets to feed on. They would take it back to their nest and in a few days that colony would be history.

On the next flight I dropped a small amount of the poison and three cans of cat food. The expert told me that should last at least three weeks. I told Don the expert advised changing the cat food mix every few days so it didn't get rancid.

Don reported to me two days later, "I never had to replace the bait. The yellow jackets carried it all off the same day. I've gone through all three cans already, but do see a marked population drop." Poor guy! But now he was happy!

Snow Storm in August

Once I flew about twice as high over Coffin as usual when making a drop and emptied about half a bag of popcorn I had left in my snack pouch. I didn't say anything.

A few minutes later Don called on the radio and reported, "Bob, you won't believe this but it's snowing up here." I knew what he was talking about but everyone else on the north end must have thought he was hallucinating. I was impressed the popcorn arrived close enough for him to see it. Must have shocked him at first!

Refreshments Anyone?

I had an interesting drop on one fire. I had reported a smoke at the edge of a logging unit in the Sweet Home District. My son, Tim, was an engine foreman there.

I circled for a while to make certain someone was on the way and just as we were flying off to resume our route I heard Tim report by radio that they had arrived at the unit and were ready to hike to the smoke. I hadn't realized he was on duty that day, and certainly didn't know his engine was the closest unit.

I told Soha to circle back. I quickly searched my bag for something to drop. I had a barf bag, candy bar and a can of pop. I spotted the crew walking across the unit and had only enough time for one pass. Without any radio communication I held the bag out the window and released it when I thought it would land in front of the crew but far enough away there would be no chance of beaning someone.

The fire Tim and his crew were hiking to when the miracle pop landed. Their engine is parked on the road at the top.

I hadn't taken time to tie the bag. As it dropped away from the plane I watched in shock as the pop can separated from its "parachute," plummeting to the ground much too fast. Oh, no!

That night Tim called me from home. "Nice shot," he said. The pop can had landed in a cat berm, which softened its impact. The thin aluminum skin was not broken. He said he prudently waited for a while before opening it so he wouldn't get sprayed! They also recovered the candy bar close by. Both had landed a safe distance from the crew, who were sufficiently impressed by the feat.

I also dropped items like newspapers to lookouts on Iron Mountain and Waldo Mountain. But Coffin Mountain was my regular milk run.

Once in 1988 or 89 after my son, John, had joined me as an Observer, he located a smoke on the ridge south of Mt. Jefferson. As he was circling he noticed some hikers "working" on the lightning strike caused fire. John successfully dropped a message — and candy treat — to them thanking them for their work and assuring them that help was on the way.

A Narrow Escape

Don Junior is an artist. He gave me a wonderful ink line drawing of the original Sand Mountain Lookout with Mt. Washington in the background. It enjoys a prominent spot on my living room wall.

The unusual thing about this drawing is the history behind it. Sand Mountain was a lookout near Big Lake, south and west of HooDoo Ski bowl. In 1967 Don Senior was the lookout and Don was a six-year-old boy.

The Airstrip Fire was threatening the lookout and the family was lifted off amid the chaos and smoke by helicopter as the flames were rushing up the slope.

This was Don's gift to me, a drawing he did of Mt. Washington and the "old" Sand Mountain Lookout that burned in 1968. The drawing is done entirely with straight lines.

Don has had an interest in Sand Mountain ever since. The building didn't burn. The following year another couple was serving there and left a stove burning while they went to Sisters for supplies. The building burned.

Sand Mountain is unique as a geologic site and can easily be damaged by careless off road use. Tracks from an ATV stay on the slope for decades. An official presence is necessary to protect it from fools.

The cone, which forms Sand Mountain, is very fragile.

Don started a non-profit group named "The Sand Mountain Society," that used parts of other lookouts to rebuild the Lookout tower. Some of the material came from Whisky Peak on the Rogue River National Forest near the Southern Oregon border. As a young man I worked on a Forest Service survey crew in the shadow of Whisky Peak.

I was able to help a couple of times with the Sand Mountain reconstruction project.

Construction just started on the "new" Sand Mountain Lookout

I took Squeek with me to see the completed building when he was less than six months old. It was not a burden to carry him on my back! (Squeek and his brother are the boys who lived with me 24/7 for the first several years of their lives. This book is dedicated to them.)

I carried Squeek up to Sand Mountain Lookout in 1997.

The Sand Mountain Society has worked with the McKenzie District to supply volunteer lookouts since the late 1980s and not only protected the geologic treasure, but turned in many fire reports as well. Now they are working on another lookout building near Detroit, Gold Point.

Narcotics?

A humorous airdrop happened one year, after I had returned to my Pleasant Hill School classroom. The second Friday of October is Teacher In-service Day. All public school children have a day off so teachers can go back to school — or at least attend conferences or seminars for things that might interest them. I attended a Conference for Mathematics Teachers at a fishing resort near Glide, Oregon.

Instead of driving back by freeway we decided to return home via back roads and enjoy a sunny day. As we topped a rise south of Oakridge a huge column of smoke dominated the sky. I knew it was a big one. We had been having a dry fall and strong east winds.

My first view of the Shady Beach Fire.

I found out later John had located it and watched helplessly as it went from a small smoke, probably started by a careless hunter, to a conflagration. As the first personnel approached the area, flames leaped more than a half-mile, potentially trapping a ground crew driving to their assignment. John was able to warn them in time.

He and his pilot, Dave Coplin, were tossed around by the winds until they feared for their lives. The Lead Plane arrived first. (They get off the ground quickly, while the Tanker has to wait to be loaded with retardant.) The pilot reported moderate to severe turbulence. *That* means it was bad.

The "new" Sand Mountain Lookout in a summer snow. Don Allen photo.

When the first tanker arrived and made a practice run *he* reported: "Everything that isn't nailed down is now banging around in here."

The decision was made that it was too dangerous to attempt a drop — something I had never heard before. The Lead Plane reported large limbs at 7,000 feet. This was the Shady Beach Fire, until that time the largest fire in the history of the Willamette National Forest.

Over the next few weeks as thousands of firefighters and support personnel descended on Oakridge, the two remaining observers, John and Sherry were each flying several hours every day. I was called back into service on weekends, but the demands of air support still taxed the regular detection program.

Finally I was asked if I could fly more than weekends. I said it could only happen if a person from high up in the Forest Service made a request of the administration of Pleasant Hill Schools, Superintendent Dr. James Howard. I thought it would take some time. But at school the next day I was informed that I could go fly the following day and the District would cover with a substitute teacher for me.

As we were returning to the airport after a morning flight on the south zone Dave Soha and I were following Highway 58. I prepared a package to drop at the Junior High where students would be just going back to classes after lunch. I put a big Snicker bar in a barf bag and a note, which read, "If you recover this package and return it to Mr. Poet on Monday you will get another candy bar."

We passed over the athletic field at about 1,500 feet and I made the drop. I couldn't see any students still outside and therefore was a bit disappointed.

easant Hill Junior High is at the bottom. My package landed near
rd base, about center of the bottom of the photo.

On Monday a student came to me with the plastic bag. The candy bar had not been touched. He thought the note meant he would get a candy bar *if* he brought this one back to me. Instead he got another one to share with his friends.

His report tickled me. A class had been in the breezeway with their Science Teacher. They saw the plane flying low — most planes stay well above 2,500 feet around there — and watched as a small object descended, landing near third base on the baseball field.

The teacher wouldn't let anyone go to recover it, fearing it was part of a "drug deal." After class the student easily found the treasure.

Wake Up Call

You might have heard the airline pilot's description of his job. "99% sheer boredom and 1% stark terror." That almost fits being an Aerial Observer. There was a great deal of paper work before, during and after each flight. There were weeks on end when each flight was three to five hours of nice scenery but no action. We flew from about 4,000 feet near the forest boundary to almost 8,000 feet near the crest on most flights. It got warm. It was easy to be lulled into sleepiness by the drone of the engine.

Old timers tell of an Observer and his pilot waking up after a nap to find they were far from the crest in Eastern Oregon. I don't know if that really happened. But it could have.

I never went to sleep. But I did get sleepy on occasion. One had to work at being alert when there had been no fires for days or even weeks. One morning I had flown an early route after a good electric storm. It was *not* a sleepy flight. But on our second trip in late morning it was warm and both the pilot and I were tired. The clouds had cleared and we were flying east from Detroit, toward Mt. Jefferson. Nothing had happened. I wouldn't say I was bored — I seldom get bored. But I was tired.

Suddenly there was a "bolt out of the blue!" A huge streak of lightning lit up the already bright morning in front of the plane. *Right* in front of the plane. Less than 1/4 mile and maybe less than 100 meters. We both were wide-awake in a nanosecond! The pilot's reaction was to yank the stick back and to the side.

When we made a turn to check out the terrain it was clear that a cell had moved in behind us. There was a single cloud in the entire sky — right overhead.

Now according to experts, lightning is not dangerous to a small plane. Modern fuel tanks are constructed to make ignition by lightning virtually impossible. But lightning *can* be hazardous to the mental and emotional health of a plane's occupants!

Pilots tell me large hail, which may accompany a storm, and especially strong downdrafts, bring the most danger. Therefore we tended to fly near a storm cell and not under one. Still, sometimes you can't identify where a cell stops. The edges may not be well defined and some storms are enormous.

Smoke rises from another lightning strike fire located on a ridge top.

Instant Fires — Just Add Water

One day Dave Coplin and I were flying just west of the Three Sisters during some limited activity. After a few minutes the intensity increased. Suddenly about 400 meters off the right wing tip where I happened to be scanning, there was a down strike and immediately flames shot out of the trees ten or twenty feet high. Coplin held steady as I oriented the map and began to work up a legal. About thirty seconds later while I had my nose in the map book Coplin let out a yell. I looked up and there were flames in the trees about 200 meters from the first smoke.

OK. Now I had two smokes to report. Back to the map book. This was repeated until we had six fires on the same ridge, all very well defined by flames as well as heavy smoke.

But the sky was getting darker and there was evidence of hail off to our left. We decided it was time to retreat. It was standard procedure to not go where either the pilot or the observer felt uncomfortable. I already had the fires plotted anyway, though not yet called in. I *never* wanted to go where any pilot was nervous about going!

We had not quite completed our 180-degree turn when there was a flash. (With the engine noise you couldn't hear thunder. I swear I heard *this* shot!) Coplin's eyes got big and he turned enough for us to see behind us. Below our tail was a huge ball of fire just like the ones we had seen on the ridge. He told me later the strike very likely would have hit us if we had not turned when we did.

We lingered a few miles away for a few minutes and watched

the rain and hail come down. When things cleared we retraced out flight. Not a smoke was visible. It appeared the moisture had extinguished all fires.

This often happens, but some fires smolder around for a few days and when the fuel dries out enough they pop up again. That's why we search especially hard for fires for days after a storm. In my book about Imnaha, I tell about a lightning caused fire that smoldered for 28 days before I found it by beating the brush. A lookout had seen it twice about a week after the storm, but a spotter plane was unable to locate it.

For the next few days Coplin and I concentrated on that drainage, looking for residual fires on the ridge. About four days later Coplin spotted the broken top of a tree just about where the bolt of lightning had scared the wits out of us. I asked him to circle lower.

As I was examining the fresh ripped-apart tree top I could barely make out a whiff of blue down in the trees. I plotted it and turned in another smoke.

It was late in the afternoon and this was remote from any road system. The District sent a crew out early the next morning. On our mid-morning flight I made radio contact with them and determined their location. Usually a crew will say, "You are right over us." But they are in trees.

My method was to fly north/south and have them tell me where my flight path was in relation to them. Then we would fly east/west and ask the same question. That gave a crossing point — assuming I could remember *where* we had crossed our own path. After doing this I was able to give the crew an idea of how far and what direction they had to go.

It is interesting that folks on the ground often mistake how difficult it is to locate them. Contrary to what Hollywood wants you to believe, hiding from an aircraft is simple. Get under *any* tree and stand still. The airborne personnel are looking for an object just larger than a hat. The person on the ground is looking at a vehicle several times as big as an automobile! No contest.

A unique view of 286-foot tall Salt Creek Falls. Highway 58 is at bottom left with several vehicles.

On the afternoon flight we repeated the process. They were much closer but still several hundred meters away. I told them to continue up the ridge and I would be back.

At the end of our route we returned. This time the crew was easier to find. I spotted helmets below the trees. I told the foreman to continue another 100 meters in the direction they were going. There was strong doubt in his voice. I could no longer see smoke, but the broken top tree was fairly easy to find.

We circled for just a few minutes until the radio crackled again. "We're at the fire. How did you find this thing? It's only five feet in diameter." What a kick that gave me!

It was satisfying to find a fire. For years there had been a strong rivalry between lookouts and aerial observers to be the first to spot smoke. I hope Ron Kintzley writes a book someday of his experiences. He is legend among Aerial Observers! And he is a great storyteller. One trick he admits to using is finding a fire and disguising his intentions from lookouts tracking him by not circling right over the smoke.

Then he might key the mike to keep a lookout from being able to contact the dispatcher until Ron was ready with his report.

Stealing A Smoke

Once I found a smoke less than a mile south of Waldo Mountain Lookout. Waldo wasn't always staffed, so I wasn't sure there was anyone there. Found out later there was. He had a straight shot at the smoke. But I will admit I had a gigantic advantage. I could circle it. Dave Soha and I could only see the small blue column when we were looking directing toward the morning sun. For the remaining part of the circle it disappeared.
Advantage aircraft.

The smoke located just south of Waldo Mountain Lookout near Cupid Mary Mountain.

Don Allen, Roxie Metzler, Sherry, myself and — the second year — my oldest son, John, helped to break down the rivalry and bring a new spirit of cooperation to detection. Roxie was the lookout on Huckleberry Mountain. Competition can be helpful. But when a fixed position lookout is looking a long way out it's nice to be able to have the strength to ask a person in the aircraft to check it out.

Also Don would on occasion ask me to fly out a given azimuth from Coffin and when I arrived miles away he would say, "What's the name of the mountain in front of you. It's off my maps." That allowed him to learn geographic names and increase his database of terrain.

Roxie's home was Huckleberry Mountain Lookout just north of Oakridge.

He and Roxie helped us by keeping an eye on our position and warning of military craft. More about that later. They also gave us ideas of where extra lightning had been located overnight. Try getting *that* information while in an airplane!
Advantage lookout.

It was a good day when we found a fire. It was an exciting day when we had a storm and found three or four. Sometimes we wouldn't find that many in a month! I don't think I had ever found more than four or five in an entire day of flying.

Setting A Record

That all changed one August morning. There had been heavy lightning activity overnight east of Oakridge. Both Patrol Planes were sent up at daylight to the south end.

Sherry chose to go south of highway 58. I was to cover the area from there to the McKenzie. I never got farther north than Waldo Lake! It was like an old-fashioned turkey shoot, I think. See, I never saw one of those...

Dave Coplin and I would see a smoke and fly a couple of miles to it. While Coplin circled I worked up a quick legal. As I was busy with the paperwork Coplin would spot another one. We were never overwhelmed, but kept busy for the entire morning flight. We would leave an area just south of Waldo Lake and check out a smoke on the east of Waldo. Then we would see another just south of the lake and go back to the same area for a new fire start.

Once I was turning in the first of six smokes to the southwest of the lake and the overworked dispatcher said, "We'll just lump them together as one incident." OK. But it cut my total by *five* smokes. (Smile.)

Waldo Lake looking northeast. Middle Sister and South Sister are to the left. North Sister is behind Middle Sister. From the north end of Waldo to South Sister is 26 miles. To the right is Broken Top.

Still, in that area of only a few square miles I turned in 25 fires that morning. I think all were staffed by late afternoon. In other words, none turned out to be false alarms.

Years later with highly advanced electronic gear Dave Coplin and an Observer on the Umpqua National Forest turned in 85 fires in one day. We did it the old fashioned way!

Front Page Pictures

When we returned to Mahlon Sweet we had a surprise. The Register Guard had requested that the Forest Service allow one of their photographers to ride in the afternoon. (The morning flight would have been *much* better. Less residual smoke and more fires to report.)

Still, I found nine more smokes — 34 for the day. That was by far a modern day record. But my passenger was not smiling. The poor man got airsick early on. And with the extra smoke in the air and the circling we did trying to locate fires accurately in terrible visibility, it was no wonder. He dutifully came up from the barf bag every once in a while and clicked off a few shots. Coplin kept a running record for me of his episodes.

Once I turned and suggested he might want to get a photo of the large helicopter dropping water on a fire near Highway 58. His face came out of the bag long enough to do so. Then on the way back in to Eugene we saw a dark smoke column in the distance. I asked Dave to cheat over that way. When we could see it was the train trestle over the Willamette River in Glenwood I "woke up" the photographer to suggest another photo Op. He complied.

This man was a trooper! Not once did he complain. Not once did he ask how long before we headed back in. Not once did he interfere in any way with our work. I really felt sorry for him, though.

The next morning the front page of the Register Guard had two large photos. Front and center was one taken from 85 Golf of the burning trestle. On the lower part of the page was a picture of a twin bladed helicopter dropping water on a fire — as seen from above, also from our platform!

That was one of my most satisfying days in the detection program. I turned in a lot of smokes, all of them were good legals, and as far as I know all smokes were eventually staffed. It was a very good day.

The observers and lookouts continued to pick up smokes from that storm each day for more than two weeks.

Meteorite Fire?

One day when the fire danger was high enough to call for two half-forest flights John and I were the Observers. He took the south half with Dave Coplin while Dave Soha and I went north. That was the flight I usually took when given a choice. Even though the fire danger was high, we had found nothing for quite some time.

While on patrol it was required that Observers give 15-minute check-ins to Dispatch with location and direction of travel. When two Observers were up the pilots often carried on long conversations over their aircraft radio frequency. The two Daves were doing so this day.

Suddenly Soha turned with a shocked look on his face and started scanning out my window and to the front. Dave Coplin had just witnessed a meteorite in broad daylight, northeast of their position. That's where *we* were!

Shortly Dave heard a report on the pilot's channel of a meteorite sighting by someone near Lebanon. The report put the fiery path to the southeast. *We* were southeast of Lebanon!

Within moments another report came from Bend of several flaming objects to the west. We were west of Bend! Reports even came from as far as Cottage Grove. All of these reports — from the public and possibly from other pilots — reported multiple paths.

Wow! 85 Golf was just about in the center of these reports. I was frantically scanning all directions. Shucks. Didn't see a thing. Now the flight was a more wide-awake experience, though.

As I said, John was flying a few miles to the south. His flight path would take him very near to where I had been just as the reports first came in. Sure enough, when he arrived in the area west of the Sisters about twenty minutes later he picked up a smoke. I was a little jealous.

Middle Sister. John's "meteorite fire" was below the position of the camera in this photo.

The interesting part came later. When a ground crew got to the site the following day they reported it was far from any trail, no roads and extremely dense forests. In fact, they said it was difficult to navigate because the trees were so close together. No sign of lightning. (There had been no lightning activity in that area for weeks and weeks.) Also, no fiery crater.

Did a meteorite start the fire? The Dispatchers did not accept the suggestion! I certainly don't know if it is even possible. But there was *no* logical explanation for this fire start, and it was very close to the center of all reports of fiery objects. Maybe someone will let me know some day.

This incident did make an otherwise humdrum flight interesting and memorable!

When Is A Smoke Not A Smoke?

One day after several weeks of no activity I spotted a smoke on an early morning flight. I was tickled, but barely had time to get a good plot when it died down. I called it in and while I was still up on the route Eugene Dispatch called me on the radio and told me an engine crew had found my "smoke." It was a caterpillar tractor at a logging site as it started up in the morning. (They put up a lot of smoke when a cold engine first fires.)

I received some grief for that one, but it still made me feel good that I was able to "get a legal" on a cat! One afternoon I had the same kind of experience. The obvious smoke didn't hang around long enough for me to get a fix. And there were no roads that near the crest. I lost it.

The "smoke" is a bit thin and has a strange color, but I thought it would be a good report.

Alas. The trail crew had been busy with dynamite near Kuitan Lake, June 27, 1988.

A few afternoons later and not far away I spotted another one. I took a picture this time, just to prove I had seen some honest to goodness smoke. Then I quickly worked up a legal and turned it in. A short time later Jon Skeels, the Dispatcher, called and told me there was a trail contractor working there. I had seen a dynamite blast. He chuckled a bit even over the radio.

A week or so later I stopped by the dispatch office and showed the crew there some of my pictures. When Jon got to the one of my dynamite "smoke" he was excited. *"Wow! Which fire was this?"*

Jon Skeels wanted to know which "fire" was captured in this photo.

Now I got to chuckle. "Don't you remember? That was my dynamite blast." He didn't give me any more grief about turning in weird smokes. Of course, he continued to give me a bad time about other stuff! (All in a very good-natured way.)

The Climbing Public

I mentioned how difficult it is to see something as small as a person on the ground while flying, especially over forest areas. But I have been surprised on occasion. Twice I saw climbers on the rocks near the top of Mt. Washington. One time it appeared to be a climbing class.

A climber on Mt. Yoran.

Another time I saw a light colored spot on Mt. Yoran, a rocky peak near Diamond Peak south of Highway 58. I asked Dave to check it out. There were two human beings looking back at us.

*Whoa! There are **two** at the very top. Trust me.*

An enlargement of the two climbers.

Probably the most unusual "climbers" we saw were near The Husband, south west of Middle Sister. We were flying south along Linton Meadow when Soha said, "What is that?" Visible against the dark rock was a patch of color. We had to investigate.

As we circled, there below us was a couple. What was strange? They didn't look at us. They were in a world of their own. My theory has always been the guy had chosen that afternoon on this rocky point to propose to his girl. What else could have kept them from curiosity about an airplane invading their quiet solitude?

For instance, when Dave took me into Jefferson Park, a popular camping area just north of Mt. Jefferson, we got lots of arm waving and attention from campers happy to see a sign of civilization. Invading their wilderness experience *never* brought shaking fists or frowns. The smiles were obvious from way up in the airplane.

This couple was concentrating on present company so completely they acted like we weren't even there. (Tough. It's a noisy airplane!) Dave and I discreetly moved off and continued our route.

Flying Is Scenic — and Fun

When the job began to get day-to-day, I would remind myself how fortunate I was to be there. I was being paid to fly over some of the most beautiful country in the world. The route we flew on a full forest flight covered about 100 miles of the Cascade Mountain crest. Our path went from just north of Mt. Jefferson in the north to well past Diamond Peak in the south. Right in the middle were the Three Sisters.

10,358 foot South Sister, looking SW. The snowfield is at least a 1/4-mile across! Note the lake to the right. I have been told it is the highest lake in the United States.

Once Dave took the plane up higher than our usual altitude as we were flying south along the crest. By the time we arrived at South Sister I was looking down at it.

That was an especially interesting view since I had recently hiked to the top with a group of high school students from Mitchell, Oregon, where I taught for the school year 1985-86. The Superintendent/Principal, Mike Carroll, took students on a special trip each summer. Flying was certainly a much easier method of seeing the top!

Looking north across South Sister to Middle Sister and North Sister. Visible beyond are Mt. Washington, 3 Finger Jack, Mt. Jefferson and Mt. Hood.

We flew over some of the prettiest wilderness lake country in North America. Hundreds of small ones and one huge one, Waldo Lake. Waldo is so clear you can often see the shadow of a boat on the bottom of the lake from 2,000 feet above the surface.

Wilderness designation kept us above 1,500 feet over that body, but one day a report from the public said there was a fire along the edge of the water. Nothing more. Eugene called me on the radio and asked me to go down as low as I felt comfortable and check out the entire shoreline. Wow! (See photo page 18.)

Dave took us down and for the next 10 minutes I was treated to some of the most fantastic scenery I had ever seen. We covered it well. The water was clear and blue. The sky was clear and blue. I was getting a view of the Lake that no one else had the opportunity to see. I was so fascinated that I forgot to take out my camera! But I'm sure it would have been disappointing. There is no way a camera could have captured that ever changing panorama and done it justice!

Two other "fun assignments" come to mind. The first was on a prescribed burn. Early every summer we helped with control burns by giving the Burn Boss a bird's eye view of his project. Often we were able to check them for days afterward and save the district from sending a patrol all the way out to look for smokes days after the fire was "out." Hose lays and equipment like fold-a-tanks were left in place for emergencies. But crews were sent to the next unit to burn as soon as the fire was mopped up inside the lines a safe distance. Overhead still worried. We helped alleviate that concern.

On one active fire the Burn Boss asked me if I could check out their west line. Smoke was keeping the ground personnel from seeing well and they were concerned the trees at the edge might have fire in them.

I told Soha what they wanted. It was a very steep unit, which fell away into a wide drainage at the bottom. This lent itself to a great way to see the unit well.

Dave started at the top and made the plane "dirty." That means he put the flaps down, kicked the rudder to the stops one way and we "flew" in a very inefficient manner — very slowly — down the steep slope. I just looked out my side window as if I was in a slow elevator and watched the trees slide past. We did that a couple of times and I was able to give the foreman a clean bill of health. *That* was fun.

Other times I spotted smoke in the tops of trees outside of the prescribed burn where it was not visible to those on the ground.

Once when Dave Coplin was my pilot and we were near Detroit Lake, the District radioed that a report had come in of a person calling for help, yelling — in a roadless area just west of the town of Detroit, above Detroit Lake.

This was a similar, but *much* larger version of the burn unit. The slope was steep and there was the big lake at the bottom from which to recover and circle back to altitude.

Coplin flew "dirty" down that slope four times. If there was a person in trouble anywhere along the mountainside I feel confident they could have made themselves visible. We were able to give it a thorough going over. It was an enjoyable ride and gave me a feeling of a job well done.

Mt. Jefferson in late summer.

The Cabot Fire

Basically the crest is the border between the Deschutes National Forest and the Willamette. Patrol Planes did not cross this border unless given specific permission.

When lightning started a series of fires on the east side near the crest and some of them joined together to become the Cabot Fire just south of Mt. Jefferson I had occasion to cross. It was easy to give an update via radio to Central Dispatch, located in Prineville. They got information when Air One was busy or not up.

One afternoon the fire was kicking up pretty well and Air One was working far to the south. They asked for an update. Wow. That fire was going.

Normally it was very unusual to be able to see flames from the air. A bit of orange color raised the excitement level a lot. This time I was clicking pictures like mad because there were huge flames. Then it got more exciting and I was running out of film!

The blowup was reaching dramatic proportions, when I was informed a jumper crew had recently landed at the top of the slope in a meadow as the terrain flattened. I contacted them on the radio and warned them about the wall of fire heading their way. The jumper thanked me for the heads up.

It wasn't really as dangerous as it sounds because even though the fire was burning intensely it was moving slowly. In fact, instead of racing up the slope and then cooling down, fuel on the slope was being consumed. Later a jumper told me that large trees were gone.

I took photos two weeks later of what had been a heavy patch of large fire. It was transformed into what appeared to be a burned over grass meadow. Live trees had been completely consumed, not a common occurrence at all.

Cabot Fire, near Mt. Jefferson. The trees are 150' tall according to one of the smokejumpers.

The fire is starting up the steep slope to the right.

Smokejumpers had just landed a few hundred yards away at the top of that slope.

24

To give some perspective, the jumpers told me the trees in these photos are 150 feet tall! I had never seen that kind of flame length.

The flames are so intense that large live trees were consumed.

I am proud of the fact that enlargements of some of these photos hung for a while in the hall outside the Regional Forester's office in Portland. One day I got a call from a man who asked permission to include my pictures in the National Archives in Washington, D.C., to represent the fires of that year.

The fire starts up the slope where Smokejumpers have set up, unaware of its intensity.

Sharing the Air

When I first started I was always in the back seat, to learn. That was fine. I had been in the back seat of an observation flight for the first time on the Rogue in 1967. I went up again in the late 1970s. I had dropped by the airport with the family on a day off from Imnaha. That was my first "solo."

I tell about that adventure in my Imnaha book. I found the smoke, returned to the airport, drove to the guard station, took my fire truck and youngest son, Dan, drove to the trail head and hiked into the wilderness to successfully locate the fire I had reported a couple of hours before from the plane. Don't know of any other observer that did all of that!

On my very first flight on the Willamette we were cruising along near the crest. The pilot and observer were carrying on a conversation in the front. With engine noise it was difficult to follow what they said. I just looked around. Then I noticed another light plane behind us a long way off.

I continued to glance back as it gradually worked its way closer and closer, behind and just to the right of us. I couldn't see the pilots face well, but it was obvious he was watching us — knew we were there.

I finally tapped our pilot and asked who it was. The reaction surprised me. He was shocked and angry. He whipped the plane to the left and dove away to increase the distance between planes. He said that was a major violation of pilot etiquette to come up from behind in a blind spot, and was very dangerous.

The Willamette National Forest has a major military flight path passing north/south right through the middle. Aircraft practice low level bombing runs, often coming ashore near Coos Bay, flying low to get under radar. Then they follow the terrain, turning north somewhere near Roseburg to fly a couple hundred miles before scooting over the crest and working their way to the bombing range near Boardman in northeastern Oregon.

I have a photo, which is buried in a huge stack of slides. I often saw the planes far below, but that was the only time I had the camera ready and caught one. I believe it was an A-6 attack plane, silhouetted against Cougar Reservoir on the Blue River District. He was right on the deck. *Way* down there.

Don Allen, this time on the "new" Sand Mountain Lookout.

Sand Mountain. The lookout is just right of center.

Another time I was lower and spotted a similar plane in the same area. Against the forest they were hard to see. Over the water it was easier. In this case when he got to the dam he dove and continued down the canyon very low. When he reached the north side of the McKenzie Valley he climbed up and over the ridge there, skimming the trees.

Very impressive.

We often saw military aircraft more than once a month. Their path was always south to north. We couldn't hear them. The lookouts did. Often the first report was from Warner Mountain in the southern part of Oakridge District. Then they had to get by Roxie Metzler on Huckleberry Mountain just north of Oakridge. If military aircraft got that far without notice, they never got past Don on Coffin Mountain.

He followed our progress whenever we were flying; from radio check-ins and binoculars. Then he kept us aware of any aircraft passing and it's approximate altitude. Once he called on the radio and there was strain in his voice. He quickly said, "Bob, Military plane at 5,500 feet just passed me going north." He knew where 85 Golf was. I glanced at our altimeter, which read 5,600 feet and noted we were flying northwest — toward a possible intercept. I told Soha and we both started scanning to the left as he climbed. After about a minute we began to relax, as it seemed the two aircraft had already passed each other.

Suddenly Dave pulled back on the stick and put 85 Golf into a steeper right turn climb. The fighter passed beneath us. Both of us feel that without Don's warning and our climb it might have been too close for comfort. As it was, Dave told me any closer and he would have been forced to turn it in as an "incident."

He explained to me his turn to the right was to exhibit as much of our plane to the sight of the other aircraft as possible. He also said with his electronic gear that pilot probably knew where we were long before Don had called us. But he probably wouldn't have done anything to save us from being startled — only colliding. I thanked Don for the "heads up."

Other types of flying bodies we shared the sky with were Helicopters, Smoke Jumper aircraft, Lead Planes and Retardant Tankers. Normally we stay as far apart as possible. No one concentrating on the ground wants to worry about other airplanes. When I reported a smoke, if it grew rapidly and a crew asked for retardant, it might be 30 to 45 minutes before it arrived. Usually it came from Redmond, but sometimes they were on other fires or even out of state. Then we would try Medford, with was closer for fires on the Willamette south of Oakridge.

A "Heavy" works on a fire just west of Oakridge in 2002. This firefighter was carrying about 2,200 gallons of water from the nearby Willamette River.

Once there was a relatively small project fire just northwest of Oakridge. My son, Tim, was part of a Sweet Home crew dispatched to it, and they had been running retardant planes that afternoon. Soha and I were at the end of our flight and had to pass about 5 miles to the south of the fire on our way back to Eugene.

Dave kind of drifted that way a bit, making sure to stay a discreet distance from the air activity. But with my telephoto lens I was able to get some shots of the Lead Plane and one Tanker drop.

This was a retardant drop on the fire west of Oakridge.

A New Perspective on Fire

At Imnaha I had been on many fires, from little tiny ones I put out in minutes to project fires several thousand acres in size and requiring weeks and thousands of personnel to control. Now I was able to view fire activity from the relative comfort of an airplane.

I say relative because the air currents were often pretty extreme near fires and I have felt the radiant heat from a fire when I opened the window. That amazed me. We were hundreds of feet away and at the altitude outside air temperatures were usually pretty cool. Yet I could easily feel the radiant heat!

Some of these fires were in the wilderness and I seldom saw more than a fire shirt or two on the ground. But with fires near roads we could see the placement of equipment.

Once I located a fire next to Highway 58 just west of the road to the airport. Soha put the plane in a very tight circle and we stayed like that for a long while. I kept giving situation reports to the Dispatch Office and ground personnel.

I was able to warn them when the fire had worked its way up the slope and was threatening homes on Airport Road. An engine immediately drove back around to attack the flames from the top and protect the structures. That was satisfying.

After what seemed like a *long* time I asked Dave to circle to the left so I could "unwind" a bit. I looked past him out of the left window awhile. I had a major kink in my neck from searching out the right side window, looking almost straight down. Must have seemed strange to folks on the ground with us in that position. It seemed strange to me. I felt a bit dizzy, but not sick, thankfully.

Smoke

In the brief span of three years one huge change in our job occurred. The State of Oregon was getting into Smoke Management in a big way. Somehow they found out what we were doing all summer, probably about the same time they enlisted the aid of lookouts. They wanted us to help monitor the movement and severity of smoke. I took many photographs on some trips and made notes of unusual smoke conditions on every flight.

I never ceased to be amazed at the haze in the Willamette Valley. It was difficult to notice on the way out. But when we returned to Mahlon Sweet there was always a layer of crud in which to descend. Obviously when there was field burning it was much worse.

Field burn plumes near Coburg, north of Eugene.

Most of the time it rose to about 4,000 feet. Sometimes it was up to 6,000 feet or more. Once I rode backseat with John and Jay Lohner when we flew a special mission toward Mt. Jefferson in smoke so thick that we were "lost" for most of the trip, even flying at 8,000 feet.

Being familiar with the maze of logging roads on private timberland just west of the National Forest helped on that trip. Jay announced he wasn't sure where we were. We could see straight down but spaghetti roads didn't help much.

The Daves and I had flown this way too many times. I told John we would see Detroit Lake off to the left in about two minutes. In about two and a half minutes it showed up. Good guess, huh?

Mt Jefferson began to show when we were only five miles away.

Typical forest terrain SW of Detroit, Oregon.

Yours truly with 85 Golf.

Passing The Torch

At the end of my first season I took my son, John, on a flight with me. That was legal because he was still an employee of the Forest Service in Prospect, Oregon. The following June he joined me in the Detection Program on the Willamette. That was a *great* year!

John quickly became an outstanding Observer. A lot of his success came from the vast experience he had with fire on the ground, especially burning units in southern Oregon. He had as a teacher, one of the best in the business, Ira Rambo.

That second year was great. We didn't see each other often, but it was nice to communicate in the air and have the thrill of flying over the forest in common.

By the third year John was ready to become Lead Observer. He was a full time employee at Lowell, as was Sherry. I was a temporary. It doesn't work well to have relatives in a supervisory roll. Therefore I was asked to move to Eugene Dispatch and sit in a chair. Maybe I will write about that one day.

Shortly after I left the Detection program was drastically cut. I would not have been happy flying only a couple of times a month.

Staffing the radio console at Eugene Dispatch was an exciting job during lightning storms. It was like being on the bridge of Star Ship Enterprise. As with the Aerial Observer's job, there were long periods of routine for every exciting bit of drama.

7,841' Three Fingered Jack and 7,794' Mt. Washington.

I had lots of helpful experience for that position; as a grunt on the fireline, a crewboss, an engine foreman, a lookout and an aerial observer. For years I thought I would still be fighting fires on the ground when I was 60 years old! When I got to be 60 it was clear that would not have been a good idea!

I met many super people as an Aerial Observer. Many of them I only talked with and seldom, if ever, saw in person. I continued that relationship after moving to Dispatch. There I spoke with lookouts and field personnel daily on the radio.

Once after retiring I was at the Jerry's store in Springfield talking to someone. A man stopped and turned, "I know you! I know that voice. Bob Poet!" I didn't recognize *him* until he spoke. We had many conversations over the years via radio.

Don left Coffin and worked almost full time on the Sand Mountain restoration and then staffing it during the summer with volunteers. He started the Sand Mountain Society, a successful organization that helped.

Ann Amundsen took over and helped carry on the excellent tradition of Coffin Mountain Lookouts. She not only sees smoke well, she also has excellent skills in communicating status to dispatchers and crews.

An interesting thing happened in about 1992. I had taken a math class on a field trip to Eugene Dispatch in early October. As I brought the students in the Supervising Dispatcher said, "Bob, Ann was trying to contact you the other day."

I went to the radio and called her. The students were "all ears"

as Coffin responded with something like, "Hi, Bob. I thought you might like to know that a few evenings ago I was hiking down below the lookout and found a bagged Register Guard newspaper that you had dropped to Don." She gave me the date, somewhere in 1987 or 88.

Coffin Mountain, looking south southwest. The repeater radio towers are at the (south) end.

I *hope* it was from the "carpet bombing" exercise, rather than an attempt to get *one* paper in the right spot. They sometimes missed by a bit.

After "retiring" from the Aerial Observing position, I often visited lookouts via roads and trails. In 1997 I hiked in to see Ann, taking Squeek with me. He won't remember the trip but he certainly was looking around at everything.

Squeek waits patiently on my back while I take a photo of a Washington Lily beside the trail to Coffin Mountain Lookout.

Squeek relaxes on Ann's bed after a "hard climb" up the mountain.

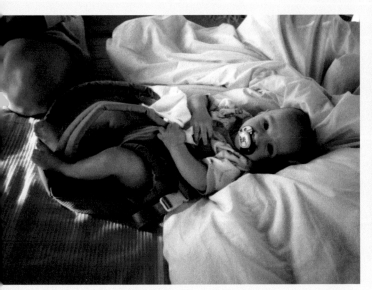

Like always, Squeek keeps an eye on Papa and his camera.

frugal because film cost money and mistakes were expensive. Now mistakes go in the trash without costing a penny.

A "Heavy" fills his bucket from the Willamette River west of Oakridge in 2002.

Ann still works on Coffin during summer fire season. I last visited her there at the end of the 2004 season.

Roxie Metzler was on Huckleberry Lookout for years. She was a high school English teacher in Springfield and still works as a substitute. She is another Lookout with an amazing ability to see smoke early and plot it accurately. Even in the middle of wild multiple fires, Roxie's voice shows she is calm, cool and efficient.

Lookouts develop a close community. John, Sherry and I feel blessed that they opened this fraternity to the Aerial Observers in the late 1980s.

I am surprised at the number of photographs I've found. These days I take many with a digital camera. But then I was more

Where are they now?

Dave Coplin is still doing charter flights and during fire season months he remains a pilot for the Umpqua National Forest.

Dave Soha has retired. After McKenzie he flew for Fed Ex where he stayed until retirement. He still hangs out at airports and does some recreational flying.

Jay Lohner flew for California Pacific Utilities for a few years and is now a deputy Sheriff in Eastern Oregon. He is a former student of mine from Pleasant Hill.

Al Quimby is still flying for United Airlines. I believe he lives in Springfield.

Bob Schmidt was still flying for Horizon Airlines the last I knew. He had moved to Portland or Vancouver.

Steve Heath started out as an Observer. Sherry and I came onboard as he was getting out of that position. As an Observer, he developed a love of flying and went on to get his commercial flying license and is now a pilot for Horizon Airlines.

Jim Freeman had also worked first for the Forest Service and then flew for McKenzie Flying Service. He currently flies a Citation Jet for Chambers Corporation.

Jerry Pierce is retired but still flies sometimes as co-pilot on some of the corporate aircraft at the Eugene Airport.

John Poet, my oldest son, is still working out of Lowell, now a Service Center for the combined Middle Fork Ranger District. There he is known as "JP." He works in fire as a specialist during the summer months, but his regular position now is Special Forest Product Sales Coordinator, long name for a job that requires many hats.

Sherry Bernard worked in Dispatch for a few years after her Observer days. She has retired from the Forest Service and lives in Oakridge, Oregon.

Don Allen is still working through the Sand Mountain Society to restore lookouts in the Cascade Range. He lives and works at a regular job in Portland.

Ron Kintzley retired from the Forest Service but is kept busy working for a private forest contractor, Scott Coleman, who owns Skookum Reforestation. Skookum not only supplies crews for tree planting and prescribed burning, but also has many 20-person fire crews available to State and Federal agencies during the summer.

Sarah Robertson still works for the Forest Service.

John Robison, always known as "JR," is retired and living in Springfield where he and his wife are remodeling a house, between his frequent trips to the golf course.

Thanks for sharing my experiences.

Following are just some of the "extra" photos. Enjoy.

Huckleberry Mountain Lookout, North of Oakridge.

As we circle for a photograph, Roxie takes some of pictures of us.

Iron Mountain Lookout, looking west.

We aren't that low. I have a zoom lens.

10,495 foot Mt. Jefferson in late summer.

Coffin Mountain looking southeast. Mt. Washington and the Three Sisters are in the background.

Coffin Mountain looking east southeast with Mt. Washington behind.

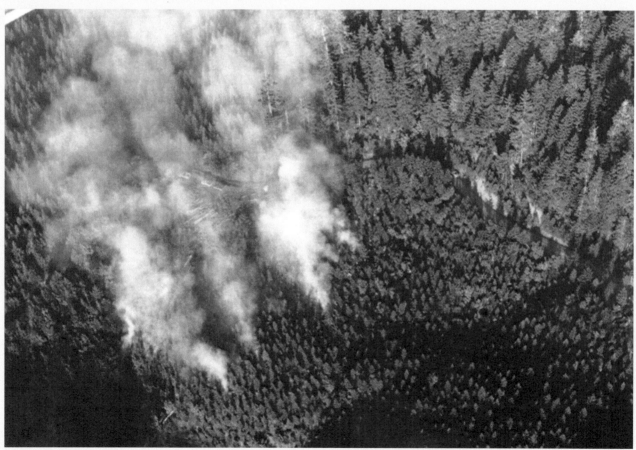

A fire in a reproduction unit.

A small unnamed pond — "No fish there. Too small," according to Soha. We called it "Campbell Soup Lake" after a retardant drop on the fire wrapped around it. A few days later it had resumed its normal color.

Ann and Bob, October of 2004. This was the last day the lookout was staffed that year.

Lookout building from the trail, October 2004.

Hiking up to Coffin Mountain in October of 2004, less than four months after shattering my left femur. The surgeons put in more than 24" of 1/2" diameter titanium rod to stabilize it.

85 Golf flies south from Coffin Mountain. Don Allen photo.

Apple Fire two hours after start. Dave Coplin photo.

Apple Fire crossing ridge top. Dave Coplin photo.

Apple Fire blowup. Dave Coplin photo.

Apple Fire crossing Panther Creek. Dave Coplin photo.

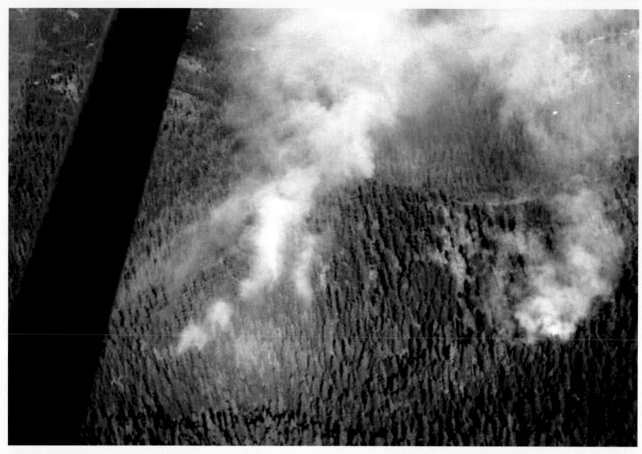

Johnson Fire, looking east. Dave Coplin photo.

Unusual view of a retardant drop. Dave Coplin photo.

Coming over a ridge to find a lightning caused smoke. Dave Coplin photo.

Smoke from an as yet unstaffed fire. Dave Coplin photo.

The Three Sisters from the west side. 10.085' Faith, 10,047' Hope and 10,358' Charity.

The Three Sisters from the south, Mt. Jefferson in the distance. Dave Coplin photo.

North Sister is near; Middle Sister pokes through the clouds to the right and behind her, South Sister. 9,175' Broken Top to the left and 9,065' Mt. Bachelor in distance. Dave Coplin photo.

Mt. Thielsen, from the west. Dave Coplin photo.

A Sky Crane helicopter at Roseburg airport. These aircraft can carry as much as 3,000 gallons of water or retardant. They can hover over a pond and fill their tank in seconds with the snorkel. Dave Coplin photo.

An unusual view of Coffin Mountain Lookout from an eye-level flyby.

Appendix (Sort of…)

Aircraft used by McKenzie Flying Service for USFS fire recon were:

Cessna 182 — N9374H
Cessna 182 — N9085G
Cessna 206 — N9150M

The "N" prefix denotes that the aircraft is registered in the United States.

The US Forest Service requirements for aircraft were:

Minimum of 230 HP engine, High wing, Long-range fuel tanks and various
Avionics installed such as a LORAN unit in those days.

The pilots and the aircraft must be FFA Part 135 qualified. This means the aircraft must meet strict maintenance requirements, like 50 and 100-hour inspections. They also have to pass inspection by both the FFA and Forest Service.

Each pilot is required to have a minimum of:

Total time in airplanes:	1,500 hours
Pilot in Command	1,200
In each category and class to be flown	200
During preceding 12 months	100
Cross country	500
Typical terrain (Low level, mountainous, etc.)	200

In addition the pilot must be instrument rated with 75 hours minimum under instruments.

All McKenzie Flying Service qualified pilots had thousands of hours more than the minimum.

McKenzie pilots flew thousands of hours on Forest Service missions without an accident or mishap. Many times this involved flying during thunderstorm activity with windy conditions and reduced visibility because of smoke or haze.

Some of the duties of the fire recon pilots before a mission:

Complete a detailed pre-flight inspection.
Make certain duty time requirements have been met and pilot is ready to fly.
If there is to be an additional passenger, make certain weight and balance is OK.
Check weather and forecast weather for the route to be flown.
Complete pre-flight briefing with the Observer.

Some of the duties of the Observer before a mission:

Check which aircraft will be used and get the correct radio equipment ready.
Collect the correct map and map book materials.
Call the Dispatch office for last minute instructions.
Check the aircraft with the pilot.
Record the beginning Hobs meter before engine start.
Install the radio equipment in the aircraft.

Pilot duties during a flight:

During the flight the pilot was required to maintain a safe altitude over the terrain and stay alert for other aircraft in the area.

When a smoke was located the pilot was to keep the Observer's field of view centered out his/her side window.

During flights near thunderstorms the pilot also had to be aware of hail potential and stay away from beneath the "anvil" of the storm.

Be aware of potential for severe downdrafts and NEVER fly up-canyon during low-level mountainous terrain flying.

Always keep an escape route out of the area that you are working. (It is easy to get busy working a fire and have weather close in behind you.)

Cross ridges at an angle and stay vigilant for severe downdrafts on the leeward side of ridges.

Always keep potential landing sites in mind in case an engine problem develops and forces an off-field landing. These may be logging roads, meadows or even shallow lakes.

The view from the "Front Office" is spectacular, but the pilot must stay alert and keep watch for other traffic and maintain a scan for smoke on the pilot's side.

Once a smoke is spotted, the pilot must help the Observer get an accurate position or "legal" of the smoke. With LORAN or GPS this is a little easier, but the pilot still must circle at various altitudes to confirm the exact Range, Township, Section and Quarter Section.

While the Observer is checking his/her legal the pilot can give him/her wind direction, estimate the height of trees, notice the slope aspect and other pertinent information.

As they are circling the fire the pilot also looks for other aircraft or smokes in the area. The pilot and Observer work as a team and after a few missions together get to know what the other is going to do and what is needed at the time.

The flights are usually three to four hours in length but the aircraft carried enough fuel for about six and a half hours. 74 Hotel had tanks large enough for over seven hours of fuel. We seldom pushed that, but on occasion did.

During times when we were working an active fire the pilot might be talking to a lead plane or tanker on the air-to-air frequency while the Observer is talking to Dispatch or personnel on the ground. During multiple fire situations the radio traffic becomes very heavy. (I had occasions when I "sat on" a smoke report for as much as 15 minutes waiting for a break to report.)

Observer duties during a flight:

Report to Dispatch every 15 minutes with location and direction of travel.

Be aware of where the aircraft is in relation to the terrain at all times. After some experience this can be done without the aid of a map.

Scan in front and to the right side of the aircraft for smokes or other aircraft.

Keep notes of any significant or unusual events. The flight path was designed to cover a strip of terrain about six miles wide.

If the Observer saw anything unusual all they had to do was point and the pilot banked the plane for a closer look. I used to tell folks who asked if I flew the plane that I had it easier than the pilot. When I wanted to deviate from the flight path all I had to do was hold my hand up and tip the palm one way or the other. The plane followed. Meanwhile the pilot had to use the yoke and rudders to make the machine react.

When a smoke was sighted the Observer started up high and made certain of the correct Township. Then as he/she began to narrow it down, the pilot flew lower until detailed information could be gathered for a smoke report to Dispatch. We never went anywhere where either the pilot or the Observer felt uncomfortable.

After giving an initial fire report we stayed in the area until the dispatcher released us or until crews arrived on the ground. While we circled we looked for additional information to help crews locate and then attack the flames. Often that might mean a nearby water source or maybe even a hazard like a fell and bucked logging unit.

Upon return to the airport record ending Hobbs meter reading.

Before leaving the airport the Observer filled out and signed the 122 form. This is what allows the contractor (McKenzie) to submit a bill to the USFS and also gives lots of material for record keeping to the folks in Dispatch.

Squeek liked to help Papa. Here he carries a load of scrap wood he has collected to Papa's pickup at a job site in 1999. Note the ever-present tongue.

Boca likes ice cream. Here he enjoys a bar on Papa's front steps in July.

Boca and Squeek in a September 2005 photo taken in Brookings, Oregon, by their Grandma.

Printed in the United States
By Bookmasters